SHARKS ARE AWESOME

by Patricia Hutchison

12 STORY LIBRARY

www.12StoryLibrary.com

12-Story Library is an imprint of Bookstaves and Press Room Editions

Produced for 12-Story Library by Red Line Editorial

Photographs ©: Martin Prochazkacz/Shutterstock Images, cover, 1; martin_hristov/Shutterstock Images, 4; Joe Fish Flynn/Shutterstock Images, 5; Aleksandar Kamasi/Shutterstock Images, 6; Michael Rothschild/Shutterstock Images, 7; Rich Carey/Shutterstock Images, 8; Ian Scott/Shutterstock Images, 9; Andrea Izzotti/Shutterstock Images, 10; Yu Yun-Ping/Shutterstock Images, 11; Gino Santa Maria/Shutterstock Images, 12; Anton_Ivanov/Shutterstock Images, 13, 29; Fiona Ayerst/Shutterstock Images, 14, 24; frantisekhojdysz/Shutterstock Images, 15, 17, 28; bearacreative/Shutterstock Images, 16; Olena Zaskochenko/Shutterstock Images, 18; Sergey Uryadnikov/Shutterstock Images, 19, 21; Willyam Bradberry/Shutterstock Images, 20; Angela N Perryman/Shutterstock Images, 22; Tropical studio/Shutterstock Images, 23; A Cotton Photo/Shutterstock Images, 25; Andrey Armyagov/Shutterstock Images, 26; Christopher Gardiner/Shutterstock Images, 27

Library of Congress Cataloging-in-Publication Data
Names: Hutchison, Patricia, author.
Title: Sharks are awesome / by Patricia Hutchison.
Description: Mankato, MN : 12 Story Library, [2018] | Series: Animals are awesome | Audience: Grades 4-6. | Includes bibliographical references and index.
Identifiers: LCCN 2016047117 (print) | LCCN 2017002177 (ebook) | ISBN 9781632354389 (hardcover : alk. paper) | ISBN 9781632355065 (pbk. : alk. paper) | ISBN 9781621435587 (hosted e-book)
Subjects: LCSH: Sharks--Juvenile literature.
Classification: LCC QL638.9 .H88 2018 (print) | LCC QL638.9 (ebook) | DDC 597.3--dc23
LC record available at https://lccn.loc.gov/2016047117

Printed in China
022017

Table of Contents

1

Sharks Are Almost Everywhere

Some sharks are gentle swimmers that dine on plankton and small fish. Others swim like torpedoes and attack their prey with huge, sharp teeth. Some bask in warm, shallow coastal waters. Many dwell in the deep, dark ocean. Sharks are everywhere.

Sharks have adapted to living in all kinds of water. They make their homes where they can find the most food. Spotted leopard sharks and bonnetheads live near the coast. The water there is shallow, warm, and full of small prey. Other sharks prefer deep water. The wobbegong and other bottom dwellers skate along the ocean floor. They burrow in the sand and wait for their next meal. The famous great white

Wobbegong sharks live on coral reefs and sandy ocean floors.

prefers the open ocean. Far away from land, the water is clear but dark. Sharks that live in open waters have keen senses that help them find their prey.

Longfin mako sharks live in the western Atlantic and central Pacific Oceans.

Surprisingly, sharks do not live only in the salty seas. Bull sharks often travel into freshwater rivers. Some sharks can actually move on land. At low tide, the epaulette shark wriggles side to side over rocky reefs. It crawls around, looking for meals trapped in shallow pools of water.

Many sharks do not stay in one place. Some, such as the blue shark, spend their nights near the ocean surface. Several times a day, they dive deep into the water in search of their next meal. Tiger sharks migrate more than 1,000 miles (1,609 km) each year. Mako sharks can cross entire oceans. These migrating fish need to adapt quickly to new environments.

1,300

Number of feet (396 m) a blue shark will dive down from the ocean surface to get food.

- Sharks live in shallow to deep ocean water, wherever they can find food.
- Some sharks can live in freshwater.
- Other sharks can move on land.
- Some sharks migrate long distances to find food.

2 Sharks Have Survived Five Mass Extinctions

Sharks appeared on Earth hundreds of millions of years ago, long before the dinosaurs. And they are still here, long after the dinosaurs died out. Sharks are very adaptable and have survived mass extinctions. Scientists study the bones of animals to learn more about how they live and die. Sharks do not have bones. But they do have teeth. From their teeth, scientists have discovered almost 3,000 different species of sharks.

If there were photos of the ancient seas, you could likely pick out the sharks. Many that lived more than 400 million years ago were shaped similar to modern sharks. They had skeletons made of cartilage, and toothlike scales covered their bodies. Ancient sharks also had

It takes approximately 10,000 years for shark teeth to become fossils.

400

Age, in millions of years, of the oldest known shark tooth.

- Scientists have studied the teeth of almost 3,000 shark species.
- Ancient sharks had the same basic shape as modern sharks.
- Over time, sharks have adapted to become better hunters.

THINK ABOUT IT

How did a shark jaw make it to Kansas? Write down all of the ways you can think of.

JAWS IN KANSAS

In 2010, the huge jaw of a shark was found in the state of Kansas. It was 89 million years old. The jaw was lined with hundreds of flat teeth. Although it was 30 feet (9.1 m) long, this shark was likely a sluggish bottom dweller. It probably ate shellfish.

two sets of fins and powerful tails. Like modern sharks, they had rows and rows of teeth.

As with other creatures, sharks have evolved over time. Modern sharks have larger skulls and scent organs than ancient sharks. These features make them better hunters. With thinner, more flexible fins, modern sharks are more powerful swimmers.

Early sharks had smooth teeth with two prongs. Most modern sharks have sharp, pointed teeth with jagged edges. Unlike ancient sharks, modern sharks have teeth that are attached to flexible jaws. This helps them latch onto their prey.

These adaptations have made sharks into fearsome hunting machines. No wonder they have survived for hundreds of millions of years.

Sharks have up to 15 rows of teeth in each of their upper and lower jaws.

3

Sharks Can Be Very Small or Very Large

When people think of sharks, big, scary beasts with sharp teeth come to mind. But not all sharks are big and scary. And they don't all have sharp teeth. In fact, the biggest shark is the whale shark. It is a mild-mannered plankton eater. Sharks come in all shapes, sizes, and colors.

The smallest shark is the dwarf lantern shark. It is approximately the size of a human hand. The largest shark is the whale shark. Also the

Most whale sharks are between 18 and 33 feet (5.5 to 10 m) long.

Blacktip reef sharks have a torpedo shape similar to great whites.

largest fish, this shark is as big as a school bus. Approximately half of all sharks grow to less than 3 feet (0.9 m) long.

Many sharks have the classic torpedo shape of the great white. But some have features that are unusual. The hammerhead shark has a wide, flat nose. Many bottom-dwelling sharks have a flat shape. They look more like rays or skates. Other sharks have snouts that look like saws. Bullhead sharks have pig noses and spines on their fins.

Some sharks are gray to blend in with the surface of the water. Others are more colorful, depending on where they live. Bottom-dwelling sharks, such as the wobbegong, look like colorful rugs. Some deepwater sharks glow in the dark.

55

Approximate length, in feet (17 m), a large whale shark can grow to be.

- Approximately 50 percent of sharks are less than 3 feet (0.9 m) long.
- Hammerheads, bullheads, and some bottom-dwelling sharks have unusual shapes.
- A shark's coloring depends on where it lives.

ITTY BITTY SHARK

The rare pocket shark has only been seen by two people in the entire world. This tiny fish could actually fit in a pocket. The name also comes from an opening above its top fin. Scientists do not know what this pouch is used for.

4 Shark Babies Eat One Another

Depending on the species, sharks are born one of three different ways. Like most fish, female sharks typically lay eggs. She finds a rock and attaches the leathery egg cases to it. Water flows through slits in the sides of the case, bringing oxygen to the babies. The tiny sharks, called pups, begin to move inside. They eat up all the nutrients in the yolk sac. When the yolk is gone, the pups tear open the egg cases and swim out.

Dogfish shark eggs underwater on a red gorgonian

Some female sharks do not lay eggs. Instead, the pups grow inside the female. In some shark species, such as hammerheads, the egg is attached to the mother. The baby receives nutrition from her body, as well as the yolk. The egg hatches inside the mother. Then she gives birth to a live baby.

In other sharks, the mothers provide no nourishment. The eggs hatch inside the mother's body, and the pups quickly use up their yolk sac. Then they look around for other eggs and eat up those yolk sacs, too. The pups that survive grow very large. Some, such as sand tiger pups, are almost 3 feet (0.9 m) long when they are born.

Shark pups are born with full sets of teeth. They swim away from their mothers right after birth, ready to live on their own.

40

Percentage of sharks that lay eggs outside of their bodies.

- Some sharks lay eggs on rocks.
- Some sharks' eggs develop inside the mother's body.
- If the baby shark hatches inside the mother, it might eat the other eggs around it.

Shark pups swim away quickly before their mothers try to eat them.

5

Sharks Top the Food Chain

Like lions on land, sharks are at the top of the ocean food chain. They are superior to bony fish in many ways. Sharks' bodies have features that make them top-ranked predators.

Sharks are super swimmers. They have lightweight skeletons made of cartilage. Sharks' slim, bullet-shaped heads cut quickly through the water. The V-shaped scales on their skin allow water to flow smoothly over their bodies. Their muscles are attached directly to their skin, helping them explode into action. For instance, the shortfin mako shark can swim up to 46 miles per hour (74 km/h).

Sharks have a big bite. The upper jaws of the great white are attached loosely to the skull. Sharks can stick them out, much like humans can stick out their tongues. This helps the great white suck in its prey to get a better grip. It also lengthens the reach of the shark's huge teeth.

You can tell a blacktip reef shark by the black markings on its fins.

Sharks have very powerful jaws.

Sharks that are big meat eaters have triangle-shaped teeth. The teeth are jagged on the edges like tiny saws. These daggers can slice off hunks of flesh from prey too big to swallow whole. During all that biting, teeth often break. This is no problem for a shark. Its jaws are lined with rows and rows of teeth. If one breaks off, a new one quickly moves forward to replace it.

8

Number of days between young lemon sharks losing an entire set of teeth.

- Sharks' bodies help them swim at high speeds.
- Their upper jaws are loosely connected to their skulls.
- Sharks' jaws are lined with many rows of teeth.

THINK ABOUT IT

Not all sharks have huge, triangular teeth. Some have smaller, flat teeth. Others have tiny teeth that are not used for chewing. What do you think these sharks feed on?

6

Sharks Have Seven Senses

Sharks share humans' senses of sight, hearing, taste, touch, and smell. In most cases, sharks have even stronger senses than humans. They are some of the most sensitive animals on the planet. In their underwater world, light and sound move differently than on land. To help sharks survive, they have two additional senses.

Every creature sends out a small electrical field as it moves its muscles. Sharks have special nerve endings on their snouts that detect these signals. These sense organs are called ampullae of Lorenzini. Small pores connect to long, jelly-filled bulbs. These lead to nerves below the skin. The ampullae send

Sharks use their ampullae to sense their prey.

HAPPY HUNTING

The hammerhead shark has a broad, flat head. Because of this, it has a greater number of ampullae than other sharks. The hammerhead may look strange, but having this super sixth sense makes it a superior hunter.

1,500

Number of ampullae around the snout of a hunting shark.

- Sharks have two extra senses that help them survive in the water.
- They can sense electrical fields.
- A seventh sense helps them detect differences in pressure.
- These senses help them tell when prey or predators are nearby.

electrical signals to the shark's brain.

Sharks use this sixth sense to locate prey and avoid predators. The ampullae also work as a compass to guide sharks during migration. Scientists think this extra sense is one reason why sharks have survived for millions of years.

Along the sides of its body, a shark has another sense system. Canals below the skin lead to the surface. Clusters of hair cells sit inside the canals. When something disturbs the water, the hair cells are pushed and pulled. The shark feels the pressure and knows that something is nearby. This seventh sense gives the shark constant updates on its surroundings.

Hammerheads have widespread eyes, which helps them see better than other sharks.

7

Sharks Are Always Looking Out for Their Next Meal

Sharks have different hunting styles depending on their tastes. Some sharks, such as the whale shark, eat large portions of small prey. They take enormous gulps of water. Then they trap tiny creatures in the spongy tissue of their giant mouths.

Other sharks gobble down tons of small fish. The thresher shark uses its long tail to slap whole schools of fish. The fish float, stunned and motionless, ready to be swallowed up. When a clever leopard shark sees a school of fish, it begins to circle in the opposite direction. Unsuspecting fish suddenly find themselves swimming into the shark's gaping mouth.

Other sharks, such as tiger and great white sharks, hunt for

Thresher sharks live deep in the ocean.

Tiger sharks eat just about anything, including seals, sea snakes, squids, stingrays, birds, and more.

big game. They circle silently below their prey, blending in with the ocean floor. Hunching their backs, they lower their fins. They swim in a zigzag motion. They use their keen sense of smell to home in on their victims. The sharks open their jaws, slicing into their meal with knife-like teeth. Great whites sometimes even breach to snatch their prey.

THINK ABOUT IT

The cookiecutter shark is a small shark that leaves a round, cookie-shaped injury on the body of its prey. What size of animal do you think this shark feeds on?

1,500

Gallons (5,678 liters) of water whale sharks can filter each hour when they are feeding.

- Sharks hunt their food in different ways.
- The whale shark filters small prey from huge gulps of water.
- Some sharks gobble down large schools of fish.
- Large sharks attack their prey with huge jaws and teeth.

8

Sharks Feast on a Buffet

Like humans, sharks eat different kinds of food. Some like huge meals of tiny creatures. Others like huge meals of large creatures. Some sharks prefer smaller foods that just float into their mouths. Others like to hunt larger game. As a group, sharks will eat almost anything.

Some species of sharks are filter feeders. Megamouths fill their giant mouths with millions of tiny plankton and small fish. The water is filtered through the shark's gills, leaving the prey behind.

Slow-moving shark species creep around the bottom of the ocean. Angel sharks and zebra horns search for crusty morsels. They eat crabs, lobsters, squids, and clams. Some bottom-feeders are scavengers that eat dead carcasses and other leftovers.

Big game hunters, such as great white, tiger, and mako sharks, prefer to eat meat. They are fast-moving predators that hunt sea lions, dolphins, and other large fish. The rich fat content of their prey satisfies their needs.

Angel sharks have pointed teeth and a strong bite.

Sharks fill up whenever food is available. But they may go hungry for weeks at a time. If they are very hungry, they may start a feeding frenzy. Sharks can smell a single drop of blood from several miles away. They surround the bleeding victim. The sharks devour it in a cloud of gnashing teeth and swinging tails. Many sharks are harmed during the ruckus.

There is a lot of trash at the bottom of the ocean. When there is no food available, sharks sometimes eat old clothes, plastic bags, and other garbage. Sharks are fairly tough. Eating trash does not usually harm them in the same way it does sea turtles and other marine life.

11

Tons (10 metric tons) of food a great white shark can eat each year.

- Almost any marine animal can be a meal for a shark.
- Filter feeders eat tiny plankton.
- Bottom-feeders eat shellfish.
- Large meat eaters eat sea lions and large fish.

Great whites will sometimes breach to catch their prey.

9

Great Whites Are Massive Meat Eaters

The great white shark is the largest predatory fish in the ocean. It is named for its white belly. Rows of enormous, jagged teeth line its jaws. This giant grows up to 20 feet (6.1 m) long and weighs in at up to 5,000 pounds (2,268 kg).

A great white pup is approximately 4 feet (1.2 m) long. It is born ready to take care of itself. It swims away from its mother, already on the prowl. It hunts and eats small fish and other marine animals. Great whites are warm-blooded

Great whites are fast swimmers.

BATTLE FOR THE BAIT

Great whites are mostly loners, but sometimes they hunt together. When there is only enough food for one shark, they have a tail-slapping contest. As they swim around each other, they slap the surface of the water. The shark that slaps the most gets the prey. Great whites usually avoid biting each other because they know even just one nibble can be deadly.

Sea lions, seals, dolphins, and small whales are all part of a great white shark's diet.

and can adapt to different water temperatures. But they prefer warm, coastal waters. They live mostly near Australia, South Africa, and the coasts of the United States.

The bullet-shaped body and powerful tail of the great white help it to swim up to 15 miles per hour (24 km/h). But scientists believe great whites are more than just brawn. They are also intelligent. They have a large brain and a super sense of smell. All this adds up to make the great white a superior hunter. These sharks make quick meals of large prey.

THINK ABOUT IT

If great whites are at the top of the food chain, why are they endangered?

300

Number of teeth in a great white's mouth.

- Great whites are the biggest hunting fish in the ocean.
- As soon as they are born, they begin hunting.
- Great whites are intelligent animals.
- They prey on seals, small whales, and sea turtles.

10

Sharks Are Not Man-Eaters

Each summer, it seems, shark attacks make the news. Sometimes swimmers are bitten by sharks. They may lose limbs. Some lose their lives. But sharks do not like to dine on humans.

Statistics show that sharks are not the dangerous predators people fear. More people are injured by dogs or cars than by sharks. Lightning has killed more humans than sharks have. Humans are not sharks' preferred food. They are too bony for sharks to digest. Sharks prefer fatty animals, such as seals and dolphins.

Sometimes a shark will attack a human accidentally. To a shark, a person swimming in murky waters might look like a tasty seal. Thinking of its next meal, a shark will take

Sharks sometimes mistake swimmers for one of their favorite foods, seals.

There are very few shark attacks worldwide each year.

a nibble. Scientists call this a "test bite." Once it realizes the person is not a food source, the shark will release the human and swim away. Unfortunately, the sharks' huge jaws can do much damage. Some victims lose too much blood, and the bite is fatal.

100
Average number of shark attacks per year worldwide.

- Sharks rarely attack humans.
- Sometimes sharks mistake humans for seals.
- They will take a test bite of the person, and then often release the human.
- If people see a shark in the water, they should swim away slowly.

Sharks are not usually territorial. They swim near people, not noticing them much at all. Yet most people panic when they see a shark in the water. This can be a fatal mistake. The shark thinks the splashing is from an injured animal. It might attack, thinking it has found a good meal. It is best to swim calmly away when a shark is spotted. Usually, the shark will swim away, too.

11 Sharks Inspire New Ideas

Sharks have been swimming in the oceans for millions of years. They are tough and efficient. Scientists are studying sharks to discover new ways of doing things.

Scientists are copying how sharks' bodies are designed in order to solve human problems. Artificial sharkskin reduces friction in the water. Suits made of it can help swimmers move faster and use less energy. Some researchers are making electricity from ocean water. They use a machine that looks like a shark's tail. It was inspired by the powerful and efficient way sharks move through the water. As the "tail" moves from side to side, it captures energy from ocean waves. The energy is converted into electrical power.

Medical researchers have learned that the special scales on sharks' skin resist germs. Almost every surface we touch is covered with bacteria. Touching a surface that has harmful bacteria can cause people to get sick. Some even die.

A researcher swims with a shark.

FROM SEA TO SKY

Sharks move in the water the same way airplanes move in the air. The powerful motion of their tails creates thrust. Wing-shaped fins provide lift to keep the shark from sinking. Studying sharks may help researchers make better rudders, wings, and even jet engines for airplanes.

Scientists are making a material that has a rippled texture like scaly sharkskin. It can be used to coat surfaces to keep them cleaner. This will help reduce infections in hospitals, restaurants, and schools. Researchers are also studying other shark tissues to find treatments for viruses, cancers, and heart disease.

1993

Year researchers discovered squalamine, an antibiotic developed from dogfish shark tissue.

- Scientists are studying sharks to help solve human problems.
- The design of sharks' bodies has inspired new inventions for swimmers.
- A machine that looks like a shark's tail produces energy from ocean waves.
- Scientists have made a material like sharkskin that resists bacteria.
- Shark tissues are being studied to help find treatments for diseases.

Scientists are studying how sharkskin resists germs.

12

Sharks Help Balance Ecosystems

Sharks keep other populations of marine animals from taking over the ocean. And they clean up waste. Sharks keep the oceans healthy.

Scientists know that if sharks are doing well, the ocean is also healthy. Sharks are at the top of the ocean food chain. When they feed, they keep other populations in balance. Without sharks, the octopus population would skyrocket, for example. Octopuses would eat up all the lobsters. Many species would suffer.

Sharks prey on sick and wounded animals. They also eat dead animals they find on the ocean floor. This helps prevent the spread of diseases. It also strengthens the fish population. Only the strongest

Humans are a threat to sharks. They hunt sharks for food or for sport.

SURVIVING EXTINCTION

Earth suffered a mass extinction 250 million years ago. Scientists think this was caused by drastic changes in the ocean. Sharks play a key role in keeping the oceans healthy. Humans are sharks' biggest predators. It is important to support sharks to help the earth survive.

and healthiest fish go on to reproduce.

The ocean is the world's most important ecosystem. It produces much of the oxygen humans breathe.

A large amount of the world's food comes from the ocean. The ocean controls Earth's temperature and weather. Without sharks to keep it healthy, the ocean would suffer. Humans would suffer, too.

Orcas and other sharks are sharks' only natural predators.

20 to 100

Number, in millions, of sharks killed each year by human fishing activities.

- Sharks keep ocean populations in balance.
- They eat sick animals, helping to prevent the spread of diseases.
- Without sharks, oceans and humans would suffer.

Fact Sheet

- Scientists study fossils to learn about shark evolution. They have found some fossilized shark scales that are 420 million years old.
- Male sharks are not always bigger than females. In most species, female sharks grow approximately 25 percent larger than males.
- Some whale sharks have lived more than 100 years.
- A shark can shed and replace thousands of teeth in its lifetime.
- Like cats, sharks have a special layer of mirrored crystals in their eyes. This helps them see in low light.
- Sharp-toothed angel sharks bury their flat bodies beneath the sand. They surprise their prey with a fatal bite.
- Tiger sharks have been called "garbage eaters of the sea." They got this nickname because they eat both live food and dead carcasses.
- Orcas are also known as killer whales. This is because they have been known to kill great white sharks and other large marine animals.

- Faulty toasters kill nearly 800 people each year. This is many more people than sharks kill yearly.
- Scientists have developed a material like sharkskin that prevents algae and barnacles from building up on the bottoms of ships.
- When a shark eats a dead animal, carbon is released. This helps move carbon throughout the ocean.

Glossary

brawn
Strong muscles.

breach
To leap out of the water.

cartilage
A strong, elastic tissue in the body.

ecosystem
All living things interacting with their environment.

environments
Surrounding factors that influence the ability of a plant or animal to survive.

evolved
Changed and developed gradually over time.

extinction
The total wipeout of a species.

flexible
Able to bend without breaking.

friction
The rubbing of one surface or object against another one.

intelligent
Able to quickly acquire new skills or knowledge.

nourishment
Food that encourages growth.

territorial
Having control over a certain area of land or sea.

For More Information

Books

Discovery Kids. *Sharks: Discover Their Underwater World!* New York: Parragon, 2013.

Musgrave, Ruth. *National Geographic Kids Everything Sharks: All the Shark Facts, Photos, and Fun That You Can Sink Your Teeth Into.* Washington, DC: National Geographic, 2011.

Pope, Kristen. *On the Hunt with Great White Sharks.* Mankato, MN: The Child's World, 2016.

Visit 12StoryLibrary.com

Scan the code or use your school's login at **12StoryLibrary.com** for recent updates about this topic and a full digital version of this book. Enjoy free access to:

- **Digital ebook**
- **Breaking news updates**
- **Live content feeds**
- **Videos, interactive maps, and graphics**
- **Additional web resources**

Note to educators: Visit 12StoryLibrary.com/register to sign up for free premium website access. Enjoy live content plus a full digital version of every 12-Story Library book you own for every student at your school.

Index

About the Author

Patricia Hutchison has been writing nonfiction for children for more than 10 years. Her favorite subjects to write about are nature and history. When she is not writing, Patricia loves to travel with her husband.